W9-AZY-576
Betty Crocker®
Christmas
cookies
WILEY
Wiley Publishing, Inc.

General Mills

Editorial Director: Jeff Nowak

Manager, Cookbooks: Lois Tlusty

Food Editor: Andi Bidwell

Recipe Development and Testing: Betty Crocker Kitchens

Photography and Food Styling: General Mills Photography Studios and Image Library

Wiley Publishing, Inc.

Publisher: Natalie Chapman

Executive Editor: Anne Ficklen

Editor: Cecily McAndrews

Production Manager: Michael Olivo

Cover Design: Suzanne Sunwoo

Art Director: Tai Blanche

Layout: Indianapolis Composition Services

Manufacturing Manager: Kevin Watt

TESTED & Betty Crocker® KITCHENS APPROVED

The Betty Crocker Kitchens seal guarantees success in your kitchen. Every recipe has been tested in America's Most Trusted Kitchens™ to meet our high standards of reliability, easy preparation and great taste.

FIND MORE GREAT IDEAS AT BettyCrocker.com

This book is printed on acid-free paper. ♾

Published by Wiley Publishing, Inc., Hoboken, New Jersey

For general information on our other products and services or for technical support, please contact our Customer Care Department within the United States at (877) 762-2974, outside the United States at (317) 572-3993 or fax (317) 572-4002.

Wiley also publishes its books in a variety of electronic formats. Some content that appears in print may not be available in electronic books. For more information about Wiley products, visit our web site at www.wiley.com.

ISBN: 978-0-470-52386-5

Manufactured in the United States of America

10 9 8 7 6 5 4 3 2 1

Cover photo: Double-Frosted Chocolate Sandwich Cookies (page 55)

dear friends,

When the holiday season rolls around, we bet you can't wait to get out your cookie recipes once again. It's no wonder Christmas is the traditional time to bake these sweet treats: they're wonderful for holiday entertaining, great as gifts, simple to bake and they make the house smell heavenly!

A busy schedule makes it hard to spend hours in the kitchen (and what busier time is there than Christmas?), so we've included a chapter of easy cookies and bars. Simply take your favorite cake or cookie mix, mix it up with a few simple additions, and *voila!* fresh, hot goodies for your family to enjoy.

A holiday cookie swap is a much-beloved tradition in communities across the nation, and for good reason: in addition to spending time with friends, you can pick up a variety of sweets for your family to enjoy. In the "Cookies to Share" chapter, each recipe makes four dozen cookies or more, so there's plenty to go around. "Family Favorites" and "Extra-Special Cookies and Bars" offer goodies for everyone from the smallest cookie-munchers to your most sophisticated guests.

From Holiday Eggnog Bars to Double-Frosted Chocolate Sandwich Cookies, we have gathered all the best Christmas treats. Happy Holidays!

Warmly,

Betty Crocker

christmas cookies

contents

top ten baking secrets 6

hosting a cookie swap 9

1 easy cookies and bars 10

2 cookies to share 32

3 family favorites 52

4 extra-special cookies and bars 74

metric conversion guide 95

recipe index 96

top ten baking secrets

1. Start with the right ingredients.

Most of our recipes call for butter and/or margarine. (Some call for butter only.) Be sure to use the regular varieties of each, not the light, whipped or spreadable choices. For best results when using margarine, select one that contains at least 80 percent vegetable oil (this type of margarine will have 100 calories per tablespoon). Use all-purpose flour unless otherwise specified in the recipe.

2. Measure correctly.

Nested metal or plastic measuring cups ranging from ¼ to 1 cup are used for dry ingredients such as sugar and flour, and for solid fats such as butter or shortening. For flour and sugar, lightly spoon the ingredient into the cup, then level it off. For butter, margarine, shortening and brown sugar, spoon into the cup and pack down firmly with a spatula or spoon, then level off.

Glass or see-through plastic measuring cups are used to measure liquids. Place the measuring cup on a flat surface, and read the measurement at eye level.

3. Chill dough if necessary.

This step, especially on shaped or cutout cookies, ensures easier handling. Work with half of the dough at a time, and keep remaining dough chilled for best results.

4. Choose the best cookie sheets.

Shiny, smooth-surface or textured aluminum cookie sheets provide the best baking results. If using dark nonstick or glass baking pans, follow the manufacturer's directions, usually reducing the oven temperature by 25°F.

Cookie sheets should be at least 2 inches shorter and narrower than the inside dimensions of your oven, so heat can circulate around them. For even baking, bake cookies on the middle oven rack and bake one sheet at a time. Cool cookie sheets between batches; cookie dough placed on warm cookie sheets will spread.

5. Prepare cookie sheets as necessary.

The recipe directions will indicate whether or not to grease the cookie sheets. To grease, use shortening or cooking spray. Cooking parchment paper can replace greasing. Parchment paper, available in the grocery store near the foil, can be torn to the length of the cookie sheet and placed on the sheet, curled side down.

6. Bake a test cookie.

Before baking an entire sheet of cookies, take the time to bake a test cookie. If the cookie spreads too much, add additional flour to the dough, 1 tablespoon at a time, until dough feels a bit firmer.

If the test cookie is too firm and/or dry, fix the dough by mixing in 1 to 2 tablespoons milk until the dough holds together better.

7. Mix, bake and decorate in stages.

Most cookie doughs can be refrigerated or frozen for baking later. Store cookie dough in a tightly covered container in the refrigerator up to 3 days, or freeze up to 6 months. Once cookies are baked, cover them tightly and decorate within a few days, or freeze them and decorate when you have the time.

8. Line pans for perfect bars.

To cut bars evenly, line pans with foil. To line, turn the pan upside down. Tear off a piece of foil longer than the pan, and shape the foil over the pan; carefully remove foil. Flip pan over and gently fit shaped foil into the pan. When bars are completely cool, lift them out of the pan by the foil "handles," peel back the foil and cut the bars.

9. Freeze with ease.

Freeze baked cookies, tightly wrapped and labeled, for up to 6 months. Do not freeze meringue, custard or creme-filled cookies. Place delicate frosted or decorated cookies in single layer in freezer container, and cover with waxed paper before adding another layer; freeze. Thaw most cookies in the covered container at room temperature for 1 to 2 hours. For crisp cookies, remove from the container to thaw.

10. Store different types of cookies separately.

Store different kinds of cookies in separate containers so the flavors don't mix. Store soft and chewy cookies in a tightly covered container. Store crisp cookies in a loosely covered container.

hosting a cookie swap

A cookie swap is one of the nicest ways to entertain around the holidays: In addition to getting a wide variety of cookies for your family to sample, you can catch up with friends. Here are a few tips to make your cookie swap a success.

Choose recipes among your friends. A simple e-mail exchange can avoid too much duplication—and get everyone excited for the party!

Have everyone bake enough so each person brings home 1 dozen cookies. All of the recipes in the "Cookies to Share" chapter make at least 4 dozen cookies, so start there for ideas. Consider doubling or tripling family-favorite recipes as well.

Set a festive tone by filling your home with holiday music, décor and holiday-scented candles. An all-Christmas music radio station, or an Internet radio service like pandora.com, set to holiday music will keep the tunes rolling.

Don't forget to set out a few healthy snacks as well. Cookies are delicious, but you don't want too much of a good thing. Warm cider, tea and coffee are always good choices as well.

Consider packing some cookies to give to the elderly, or to mail to people in the military. If you're sending cookies and bars, be sure to choose sturdy ones that will travel well. The Milk Chocolate–Malt Brownies (page 44) and the Pecan Pie Squares (page 48) are good choices.

Provide each guest with printed copies of the recipes to take home. Either photocopy them from this book, or print them directly from our Web site, bettycrocker.com!

easy cookies and bars

Fudge Crinkles { 30 cookies }

Prep Time: 1 Hour Start to Finish: 1 Hour

- 1 box (1 lb 2.25 oz) devil's food cake mix with pudding
- ½ cup vegetable oil
- 2 eggs
- 1 teaspoon vanilla
- ⅓ cup powdered sugar

1 Heat oven to 350°F. In large bowl, mix cake mix, oil, eggs and vanilla with spoon until dough forms.

2 Shape dough into 1-inch balls. Roll balls in powdered sugar. On ungreased cookie sheet, place balls about 2 inches apart.

3 Bake 10 to 12 minutes or until set. Cool 1 minute; remove from cookie sheet to cooling rack. Cool completely, about 30 minutes. Store tightly covered.

1 Cookie: Calories 110 (Calories from Fat 45); Total Fat 5g (Saturated Fat 1g); Cholesterol 15mg; Sodium 140mg; Total Carbohydrate 15g (Dietary Fiber 0g); Protein 1g

{ Instead of rolling the cookies in powdered sugar, dip the tops into chocolate candy sprinkles before baking.

For extra fun, stir 1 cup mini candy-coated chocolate baking bits into the dough. }

Peanutty Granola Cookies

32 cookies

Prep Time: **1 Hour** Start to Finish: **1 Hour 45 Minutes**

- 1 box (1 lb 2.25 oz) butter recipe yellow cake mix with pudding
- ½ cup butter or margarine, softened
- 2 eggs
- 4 sweet and salty peanut granola bars (from 7.4-oz box), coarsely chopped
- ½ cup peanut butter chips (from 10-oz bag)
- 1½ teaspoons shortening

1. Heat oven to 350°F. In large bowl, beat cake mix, butter and eggs with electric mixer on medium speed until smooth. Stir in chopped granola bars. Onto ungreased cookie sheet, drop mixture by tablespoonfuls.
2. Bake 10 to 12 minutes or until set and light golden brown around edges. Let cool on cookie sheet 2 minutes. Remove from cookie sheet to cooling rack. Cool completely, about 30 minutes.
3. In microwavable food-storage plastic bag, place peanut butter chips and shortening; seal bag. Microwave on High 15 seconds; squeeze bag. Microwave 15 to 25 seconds longer or until melted; squeeze bag until mixture is smooth. Cut off tiny corner of bag; squeeze bag to drizzle mixture over cookies. Let stand about 10 minutes or until drizzle is set. Store in airtight container.

1 Cookie: Calories 120 (Calories from Fat 50); Total Fat 6g (Saturated Fat 2.5g); Cholesterol 20mg; Sodium 150mg; Total Carbohydrate 16g (Dietary Fiber 0g); Protein 1g

If you like the flavor combination of peanut butter and chocolate, substitute chocolate chips for the peanut butter chips.

Use your favorite flavor of granola bars for these cookies.

Chocolate Chip and Peanut Butter Cookies

About 4 dozen cookies

Prep Time: 55 Minutes **Start to Finish:** 1 Hour 10 Minutes

- 1 box (1 lb 2.25 oz) yellow cake mix with pudding
- 1¼ cups crunchy peanut butter
- ¼ cup packed brown sugar
- ¼ cup butter or margarine, softened
- 2 eggs
- 1 bag (11.5 oz) milk chocolate chips (2 cups)

1. Heat oven to 350°F. In large bowl, beat cake mix, peanut butter, brown sugar, butter and eggs with electric mixer on medium speed until well blended. Stir in chocolate chips.
2. Onto ungreased cookie sheets, drop dough by rounded tablespoonfuls 2 inches apart.
3. Bake 9 to 11 minutes or until edges are set (centers will be soft). Cool 1 minute; remove from cookie sheets to cooling racks.

1 Cookie: Calories 140 (Calories from Fat 70); Total Fat 7g (Saturated Fat 3g); Cholesterol 15mg; Sodium 115mg; Total Carbohydrate 15g (Dietary Fiber 0g); Protein 3g

To make drop cookies uniform in size and shape, use a spring-handled cookie scoop. Select the size of the scoop based on how large or small you like your cookies.

To soften butter, let it stand at room temperature for 30 to 45 minutes.

Butterscotch-Oatmeal Cookies

{ About 4 dozen cookies }

Prep Time: **1 Hour 5 Minutes** Start to Finish: **1 Hour 20 Minutes**

- 1 cup butter or margarine, softened
- ¼ cup sugar
- 1 teaspoon ground cinnamon
- 1 egg
- 1 box (1 lb 2.25 oz) yellow cake mix with pudding
- 2 cups quick-cooking oats
- 1 cup butterscotch chips
- 1 cup chopped walnuts

1. Heat oven to 350°F. In large bowl, beat butter, sugar, cinnamon and egg with electric mixer on medium speed until creamy. Stir in cake mix and oats until blended. Stir in butterscotch chips and walnuts.
2. Onto ungreased cookie sheets, drop dough by teaspoonfuls about 2 inches apart.
3. Bake 10 to 12 minutes or until light brown. Immediately remove from cookie sheets to cooling racks.

1 Cookie: Calories 130 (Calories from Fat 70); Total Fat 8g (Saturated Fat 4g); Cholesterol 15mg; Sodium 115mg; Total Carbohydrate 15g (Dietary Fiber 0g); Protein 1g

Both old-fashioned and quick-cooking oats are whole oats that have been steamed and rolled. Because the quick-cooking variety is cut into small pieces before steaming, it gives baked goods a softer texture.

We like using butterscotch chips in these yummy cookies, but you can try making them with chocolate chips instead.

Spicy Pumpkin Cookies

{ About 2½ dozen cookies }

Prep Time: **15 Minutes** Start to Finish: **55 Minutes**

- 1 box (1 lb 2.25 oz) yellow cake mix with pudding
- 2 teaspoons pumpkin pie spice
- 1 cup canned pumpkin (not pumpkin pie mix)
- ¼ cup butter or margarine, softened
- ½ cup raisins, if desired
- 1 cup vanilla creamy ready-to-spread frosting
- Ground nutmeg or cinnamon, if desired

1 Heat oven to 375°F. Lightly grease cookie sheet with shortening. In large bowl, mix cake mix and pumpkin pie spice. Stir in pumpkin and butter until well blended. Stir in raisins.

2 Drop dough by generous tablespoonfuls about 2 inches apart onto cookie sheet.

3 Bake 11 to 12 minutes or until set and light golden brown around edges. Cool 1 to 2 minutes; remove from cookie sheet to cooling rack. Cool completely, about 30 minutes. Frost with frosting. Sprinkle with nutmeg.

1 Cookie: Calories 85 (Calories from Fat 35); Total Fat 4g (Saturated Fat 2g); Cholesterol 5mg; Sodium 120mg; Total Carbohydrate 22g (Dietary Fiber 0g); Protein 0g

{ If pumpkin pie spice isn't handy, use 1 teaspoon ground cinnamon, ½ teaspoon ground nutmeg and ½ teaspoon ground ginger instead. If you prefer nuts to raisins, substitute ½ cup chopped pecans or walnuts for the raisins. }

Super-Easy Macaroon Chewies

About 3 dozen cookies

Prep Time: **1 Hour 15 Minutes** Start to Finish: **3 Hours 15 Minutes**

- 1 pouch (1 lb 1.5 oz) sugar cookie mix
- 1 bag (14 oz) flaked coconut
- ¼ cup milk
- 1 can (14 oz) sweetened condensed milk (not evaporated)
- ½ cup semisweet chocolate chips
- 1 teaspoon butter or margarine

1 In large bowl, stir cookie mix and coconut. Stir in milk and condensed milk until well blended. Cover; refrigerate 2 hours.

2 Heat oven to 375°F. Line cookie sheet with cooking parchment paper or use ungreased cookie sheet. On cookie sheet, drop dough by rounded tablespoonfuls about 2 inches apart.

3 Bake 12 to 14 minutes or until edges are light golden brown. Cool 5 minutes; remove from cookie sheet to cooling rack. Cool completely.

4 In small microwaveable bowl, microwave chocolate chips and butter on High 1 minute to 1 minute 30 seconds, stirring every 30 seconds, until melted and smooth. Using fork, drizzle chocolate in lines over cookies. Store loosely covered.

1 Cookie: Calories 170 (Calories from Fat 60); Total Fat 7g (Saturated Fat 5g); Cholesterol 0mg; Sodium 75mg; Total Carbohydrate 24g (Dietary Fiber 0g); Protein 2g

Carrot-Spice Cookies

{ About 4 dozen cookies }

Prep Time: **1 Hour** Start to Finish: **1 Hour 25 Minutes**

COOKIES

1 box (1 lb 2 oz) carrot cake mix with pudding

¼ cup all-purpose flour

½ cup butter or margarine, melted

2 eggs

1 cup sweetened dried cranberries

FROSTING

½ cup cream cheese creamy ready-to-spread frosting (from 1-lb container)

1 Heat oven to 350°F. In large bowl, beat cake mix, flour, butter and eggs with electric mixer on low speed 1 minute. Stir in cranberries.

2 Onto ungreased cookie sheets, drop dough by teaspoonfuls about 2 inches apart.

3 Bake 10 to 12 minutes or until edges are set. Immediately remove from cookie sheets to cooling racks. Cool completely, about 10 minutes.

4 In small microwavable bowl, microwave frosting on High 10 to 15 seconds or until frosting is thin enough to drizzle. Drizzle frosting over cookies.

1 Cookie: Calories 80 (Calories from Fat 30); Total Fat 3g (Saturated Fat 1.5g); Cholesterol 15mg; Sodium 85mg; Total Carbohydrate 12g (Dietary Fiber 0g); Protein 0g

{ Try using raisins instead of the dried cranberries. }

Peppermint Shortbread Bites
64 cookies

Prep Time: **25 Minutes** Start to Finish: **2 Hours**

- 1 cup butter, softened (do not use margarine)
- ½ cup powdered sugar
- 2 cups all-purpose flour
- 1 teaspoon peppermint extract
- 3 tablespoons finely crushed hard peppermint candies (about 6 candies)
- 1 tablespoon granulated sugar
- 3 oz vanilla-flavored candy coating (almond bark), melted

1. In large bowl, beat butter and powdered sugar with electric mixer on medium speed until fluffy. On low speed, beat in flour and peppermint extract.
2. On ungreased cookie sheet, pat dough into 6-inch square, about ¾ inch thick. Cover; refrigerate 30 minutes.
3. Heat oven to 325°F. On cookie sheet, cut dough into 8 rows by 8 rows, making 64 squares. With knife, separate rows by ¼ inch.
4. Bake 28 to 35 minutes or until set and edges are just starting to turn golden. Meanwhile, in small bowl, mix crushed candy and granulated sugar. In small resealable food-storage plastic bag, place melted candy coating. Seal bag; cut tiny hole in corner of bag.
5. Do not remove cookies from cookie sheet. Pipe candy coating over cookies. Before candy coating sets, sprinkle candy mixture over cookies. Remove cookies to cooling racks. Cool completely, about 30 minutes.

1 Cookie: Calories 50 (Calories from Fat 30); Total Fat 3.5g (Saturated Fat 2g); Cholesterol 10mg; Sodium 20mg; Total Carbohydrate 5g (Dietary Fiber 0g); Protein 0g

Fudgy Pecan Bars { 32 bars }

Prep Time: **25 Minutes** Start to Finish: **1 Hour 50 Minutes**

- 1 box (1 lb 2.25 oz) devil's food cake mix with pudding
- ⅓ cup butter or margarine, softened
- 2 tablespoons milk
- 1 teaspoon vanilla
- 1 egg
- 1¼ cups semisweet chocolate chips
- ¼ cup butter or margarine, melted
- 2 eggs
- 1 cup chopped pecans
- 1 tablespoon powdered sugar

1 Heat oven to 350°F. Spray bottom only of 13 × 9-inch pan with baking spray with flour. Measure ½ cup of the cake mix into medium bowl; set aside.

2 In large bowl, beat remaining cake mix, ⅓ cup butter, the milk, vanilla and egg with electric mixer on low speed until crumbly. Press dough in pan. Sprinkle with chocolate chips; press into dough.

3 Add melted butter and 2 eggs to reserved cake mix. Beat on medium speed until smooth. Stir in pecans. Spread mixture over crust.

4 Bake 25 to 28 minutes or until center is set. Cool completely, about 1 hour. Sprinkle powdered sugar over top. For bars, cut into 8 rows by 4 rows.

1 Bar: Calories 170 (Calories from Fat 80); Total Fat 9g (Saturated Fat 4g); Cholesterol 30mg; Sodium 160mg; Total Carbohydrate 18g (Dietary Fiber 1g); Protein 2g

If your family prefers, you can substitute cashews for the pecans.

Use a tea strainer to lightly sift the powdered sugar over the bars.

Triple-Chocolate Cherry Bars

48 bars

Prep Time: **10 Minutes** Start to Finish: **1 Hour 40 Minutes**

- 1 box (1 lb 2.25 oz) chocolate fudge cake mix with pudding
- 1 can (21 oz) cherry pie filling
- 2 eggs, beaten
- ½ bag (12-oz size) miniature semisweet chocolate chips (1 cup)
- 1 container chocolate whipped ready-to-spread frosting

1. Heat oven to 350°F. Grease bottom and sides of 15 × 10 × 1-inch pan with shortening; lightly flour.
2. In large bowl, mix cake mix, pie filling, eggs and chocolate chips with spoon. Pour into pan.
3. Bake 20 to 30 minutes or until toothpick inserted in center comes out clean. Cool completely, about 1 hour. Frost with frosting. For bars, cut into 8 rows by 6 rows.

1 Bar: Calories 110 (Calories from Fat 35); Total Fat 4g (Saturated Fat 2g); Cholesterol 10mg; Sodium 80mg; Total Carbohydrate 18g (Dietary Fiber 1g); Protein 1g

Triple-Chocolate Strawberry Bars Substitute strawberry pie filling for the cherry.

German Chocolate Bars {48 bars}

Prep Time: **15 Minutes** Start to Finish: **3 Hours 55 Minutes**

½ cup butter or margarine, softened

1 box (1 lb 2.25 oz) German chocolate cake mix with pudding

1 container coconut pecan creamy ready-to-spread frosting

1 bag (6 oz) semisweet chocolate chips (1 cup)

¼ cup milk

1 Heat oven to 350°F. Lightly grease bottom and sides of 13 × 9-inch rectangular pan with shortening. In medium bowl, cut butter into cake mix using pastry blender or crisscrossing 2 knives, until crumbly. Press half of the mixture (2½ cups) in bottom of pan. Bake 10 minutes.

2 Carefully spread frosting over baked layer; sprinkle evenly with chocolate chips. Stir milk into remaining cake mixture. Drop by teaspoonfuls onto chocolate chips.

3 Bake 25 to 30 minutes or until cake portion is slightly dry to the touch. Cool completely, about 1 hour. Cover and refrigerate about 2 hours or until firm. For bars, cut into 8 rows by 6 rows. Store covered in refrigerator.

1 Bar: Calories 135 (Calories from Fat 70); Total Fat 8g (Saturated Fat 4g); Cholesterol 15mg; Sodium 100mg; Total Carbohydrate 15g (Dietary Fiber 0g); Protein 1g

{For an easy dessert with restaurant style, place 2 bars on individual serving plates. Top with whipped cream and grated milk chocolate from a candy bar.}

Lemon Cheesecake Bars { 48 bars }

Prep Time: **15 Minutes** Start to Finish: **4 Hours 40 Minutes**

- 1 box (1 lb 2.25 oz) lemon cake mix with pudding
- ⅓ cup butter or margarine, softened
- 3 eggs
- 1 package (8 oz) cream cheese, softened
- 1 cup powdered sugar
- 2 teaspoons grated lemon peel
- 2 tablespoons lemon juice

1. Heat oven to 350°F. In large bowl, beat cake mix, butter and 1 of the eggs with electric mixer on low speed until crumbly. Press in bottom of ungreased 13 × 9-inch rectangular pan.
2. In medium bowl, beat cream cheese with electric mixer on medium speed until smooth. Gradually beat in powdered sugar on low speed. Stir in lemon peel and lemon juice until smooth. Reserve ½ cup cream cheese mixture; refrigerate. Beat remaining 2 eggs into remaining cream cheese mixture on medium speed until blended. Spread over cake mixture.
3. Bake about 25 minutes or until set. Cool completely, about 1 hour. Spread with reserved cream cheese mixture. Refrigerate about 3 hours or until firm. For bars, cut into 8 rows by 6 rows. Store covered in refrigerator.

1 Bar: Calories 85 (Calories from Fat 35); Total Fat 4g (Saturated Fat 2g); Cholesterol 20mg; Sodium 95mg; Total Carbohydrate 11g (Dietary Fiber 0g); Protein 1g

{ A whole lemon will work fine. One lemon yields 1½ to 3 teaspoons of grated peel and 2 to 3 tablespoons of juice, so you'll need only one for this recipe. }

White Chocolate–Cranberry Bars { 24 bars }

Prep Time: **10 Minutes** Start to Finish: **1 Hour 35 Minutes**

- 1 box (1 lb 2.25 oz) white cake mix with pudding
- ⅓ cup butter or margarine, melted
- 2 tablespoons water
- 2 eggs
- 1½ cups dried cranberries
- 1 cup white vanilla baking chips

1. Heat oven to 350°F. Grease bottom only of 13 × 9-inch rectangular pan with shortening; lightly flour.
2. In large bowl, mix cake mix, butter, water and eggs with spoon until dough forms (some dry mix will remain). Stir in cranberries and white baking chips. Spread evenly in pan.
3. Bake 20 to 25 minutes or until toothpick inserted in center comes out clean. Cool completely, about 1 hour. For bars, cut into 6 rows by 4 rows.

1 Bar: Calories 210 (Calories from Fat 80); Total Fat 9g (Saturated Fat 5g); Cholesterol 25mg; Sodium 180mg; Total Carbohydrate 30g (Dietary Fiber 0g); Protein 2g

These bars look especially festive when topped with white chocolate. To make white chocolate drizzle, melt ⅓ cup white baking chips and 1½ teaspoons shortening in 1-quart saucepan over low heat, stirring frequently, until melted and smooth. Drizzle melted white baking chip mixture over cooled bars. Let stand 30 minutes or until set.

Chewy Orange-Date Bars { 48 bars }

Prep Time: **15 Minutes** Start to Finish: **2 Hours 20 Minutes**

- 1 box (1 lb 2.25 oz) yellow cake mix with pudding
- ¾ cup quick-cooking oats
- ¾ cup butter or margarine, melted
- 1 tablespoon grated orange peel
- 3 eggs
- 2 cups chopped dates (from two 8-oz packages)
- 2 cups chopped walnuts

1. Heat oven to 350°F. Spray bottom and sides of 15 × 10 × 1-inch pan with baking spray with flour.
2. In large bowl, beat cake mix, oats, butter, orange peel and eggs with electric mixer on medium speed about 2 minutes or until batter is thick. Stir in dates and walnuts. Spread in pan.
3. Bake 20 to 25 minutes or until top is golden brown and toothpick inserted in center comes out clean. Cool on cooling rack 10 minutes. Run knife around sides of pan to loosen bars. Cool completely, about 1 hour 30 minutes. For bars, cut into 8 rows by 6 rows.

1 Bar: Calories 130 (Calories from Fat 70); Total Fat 7g (Saturated Fat 2.5g); Cholesterol 20mg; Sodium 100mg; Total Carbohydrate 15g (Dietary Fiber 1g); Protein 2g

{ You can chop whole pitted dates or buy chopped dates. }

cookies to share

Inside-Out Chocolate Chip Cookies { About 4½ dozen cookies }

Prep Time: **10 Minutes** Start to Finish: **22 Minutes**

- 1 cup granulated sugar
- ¾ cup packed brown sugar
- ¾ cup butter or margarine, softened
- ½ cup shortening
- 1 teaspoon vanilla
- 2 eggs
- 2½ cups all-purpose flour
- ½ cup baking cocoa
- 1 teaspoon baking soda
- ¼ teaspoon salt
- 1½ cups white vanilla baking chips
- 1 cup chopped nuts

1 Heat oven to 350°F. In large bowl, beat sugars, butter, shortening, vanilla and eggs with electric mixer on medium speed, or mix with spoon. Stir in flour, cocoa, baking soda and salt. Stir in white vanilla chips and nuts.

2 Drop dough by rounded tablespoonfuls about 2 inches apart onto ungreased cookie sheet. Bake 10 to 12 minutes or until set. Cool 1 to 2 minutes; remove from cookie sheet to cooling rack.

1 Cookie: Calories 140 (Calories from Fat 70); Total Fat 8g (Saturated Fat 2g); Cholesterol 10mg; Sodium 70mg; Total Carbohydrate 15g (Dietary Fiber 0g); Protein 2g

Marvelously Minty Cookies

{ About 8 dozen cookies }

Prep Time: **1 Hour 45 Minutes** Start to Finish: **1 Hour 45 Minutes**

- 2½ cups sugar
- 1 cup butter or margarine, softened
- ½ cup shortening
- 1 teaspoon vanilla
- 2 eggs
- 4 cups all-purpose flour
- 2 teaspoons baking soda
- 1 teaspoon salt
- 3 cups pastel-colored mint candy drops

1 Heat oven to 350°F. In large bowl, beat sugar, butter, shortening, vanilla and eggs with electric mixer on medium speed until light and fluffy, or mix with spoon. Stir in flour, baking soda and salt. Stir in mint chips.

2 On ungreased cookie sheet, drop dough by rounded teaspoonfuls about 2 inches apart.

3 Bake 11 to 13 minutes or until light golden brown. Cool 30 seconds; remove from cookie sheet to cooling rack.

1 Cookie: Calories 80 (Calories from Fat 25); Total Fat 3g (Saturated Fat 2g); Cholesterol 10mg; Sodium 65mg; Total Carbohydrate 12g (Dietary Fiber 0g); Protein 1g

Hidden Treasure Cookies

{ About 4 dozen cookies }

Prep Time: **1 Hour 15 Minutes** Start to Finish: **1 Hour 45 Minutes**

- ½ cup powdered sugar
- 1 cup butter or margarine, softened
- 1 teaspoon vanilla
- 2¼ cups all-purpose flour
- ½ cup finely chopped nuts
- ¼ teaspoon salt
- 12 caramels, each cut into 4 pieces
- Additional powdered sugar

1. Heat oven to 400°F. In large bowl, mix ½ cup powdered sugar, the butter and vanilla. Stir in flour, nuts and salt until dough holds together.
2. Mold portions of dough around pieces of caramels to form 1-inch balls. On ungreased cookie sheet, place balls about 1 inch apart.
3. Bake 10 to 12 minutes or until set but not brown. In small bowl, place additional powdered sugar. Roll cookies in powdered sugar while warm. Cool completely on cooling rack, about 30 minutes. Roll in powdered sugar again.

1 Cookie: Calories 90 (Calories from Fat 45); Total Fat 5g (Saturated Fat 2g); Cholesterol 10mg; Sodium 45mg; Total Carbohydrate 10g (Dietary Fiber 0g); Protein 0g

{ Vary the treasures in your cookies! Instead of caramels, try candied cherries, malted milk balls, chocolate-covered raisins or gummy fruit candies. }

Spritz

About 5 dozen cookies

Prep Time: **1 Hour 50 Minutes** Start to Finish: **2 Hours 20 Minutes**

- 1 cup butter or margarine, softened
- ½ cup sugar
- 1 egg
- 2½ cups all-purpose flour
- ¼ teaspoon salt
- ¼ teaspoon almond extract or vanilla
- Few drops of food color, if desired

1 Heat oven to 400°F. In large bowl, beat butter, sugar and egg with electric mixer on medium speed, or mix with spoon. Stir in remaining ingredients.

2 Place dough in cookie press. On ungreased cookie sheet, form desired shapes.

3 Bake 5 to 8 minutes or until set but not brown. Immediately remove from cookie sheet to cooling rack. Cool completely, about 30 minutes.

1 Cookie: Calories 50 (Calories from Fat 30); Total Fat 3g (Saturated Fat 1.5g); Cholesterol 10mg; Sodium 30mg; Total Carbohydrate 6g (Dietary Fiber 0g); Protein 0g

Chocolate Spritz Stir 2 oz unsweetened baking chocolate, melted and cooled, into butter-sugar mixture. Omit food color.

Rum Butter Spritz Substitute rum extract for the almond extract. Tint dough with food colors. After baking, spread cooled cookies with Rum Butter Glaze: Melt ¼ cup butter or margarine in 1-quart saucepan; remove from heat. Stir in 1 cup powdered sugar and 1 teaspoon rum extract. Stir in 1 to 2 tablespoons hot water until glaze is spreadable. Tint glaze with food color to match cookies.

Spicy Spritz Stir in 1 teaspoon ground cinnamon, ½ teaspoon ground nutmeg and ¼ teaspoon ground allspice with the flour.

After baking, decorate cookies with edible glitter, colored sugar, nonpareils, red cinnamon candies or finely chopped nuts. A drop of corn syrup will hold the decorations in place nicely.

SOPHIA

Season's Best Sugar Cookies

About 5 dozen cookies

Prep Time: **1 Hour** Start to Finish: **3 Hours**

COOKIES

1½ cups powdered sugar

1 cup butter or margarine, softened

1 teaspoon vanilla

½ teaspoon almond extract

1 egg

2½ cups all-purpose flour

1 teaspoon baking soda

1 teaspoon cream of tartar

WHITE GLAZE

2 cups powdered sugar

2 tablespoons milk

¼ teaspoon almond extract

Sprinkles

Red edible glitter or red sugar

1 In large bowl, beat 1½ cups powdered sugar and the butter with electric mixer on medium speed, or mix with spoon. Stir in vanilla, ½ teaspoon almond extract and the egg. Stir in flour, baking soda and cream of tartar. Cover and refrigerate about 2 hours or until firm.

2 Heat oven to 375°F. On lightly floured cloth-covered surface, roll half of dough at a time ⅛ inch thick. Cut into desired shapes. On ungreased cookie sheets, place shapes about 2 inches apart.

3 Bake 7 to 8 minutes or until light brown. Remove from cookie sheet to cooling rack. Cool completely.

4 Mix glaze ingredients until smooth and desired spreading consistency, adding a few extra drops milk if needed. Spread glaze over cookies. Sprinkle with sugars.

1 Cookie: Calories 80 (Calories from Fat 30); Total Fat 3g (Saturated Fat 2g); Cholesterol 10mg; Sodium 45mg; Total Carbohydrate 11g (Dietary Fiber 0g); Protein 0g

When you're making cutout cookies, always work with well-chilled dough. Cold dough rolls out smoothly, with less sticking. The cookies are easy to cut, remove and transfer to baking sheets, and they hold their shape in the oven.

To purchase edible glitter, go to sweetc.com and search for edible glitter.

Lemon Stampers

About 5 dozen cookies

Prep Time: **1 Hour 10 Minutes** Start to Finish: **3 Hours 40 Minutes**

- 1 cup butter or margarine, softened
- 1 package (3 oz) cream cheese, softened
- ½ cup sugar
- 1 tablespoon grated lemon peel
- 2 cups all-purpose flour

1. In large bowl, beat butter and cream cheese with electric mixer on medium speed, or mix with spoon. Stir in sugar and lemon peel. Gradually stir in flour. Cover; refrigerate about 2 hours or until firm.
2. Heat oven to 375°F. Shape dough into 1-inch balls. On ungreased cookie sheet, place balls about 2 inches apart. "Stamp" balls to about ¼-inch thickness using a potato masher, the bottom of a glass, the bumpy side of a meat mallet, the end of an empty spool of thread or a cookie press, dipping first into additional sugar.
3. Bake 7 to 9 minutes or until set but not brown. Remove from cookie sheet to cooling rack. Cool completely, about 30 minutes.

1 Cookie: Calories 50 (Calories from Fat 30); Total Fat 3.5g (Saturated Fat 2g); Cholesterol 10mg; Sodium 25mg; Total Carbohydrate 5g (Dietary Fiber 0g); Protein 0g

When shaping dough into balls, use a level tablespoon of dough to create a perfect 1-inch ball. For bright-topped cookies, sprinkle with colored sugar before baking.

Milk Chocolate–Malt Brownies

48 brownies

Prep Time: **10 Minutes** **Start to Finish:** **45 Minutes**

- 1 bag (11.5 oz) milk chocolate chips (2 cups)
- ½ cup butter or margarine
- ¾ cup sugar
- 1 teaspoon vanilla
- 3 eggs
- 1¾ cups all-purpose flour
- ½ cup natural- or chocolate-flavor malted milk powder
- ½ teaspoon baking powder
- ¼ teaspoon salt
- 1 cup malted milk balls, coarsely chopped

1. Heat oven to 350°F. Grease 13 × 9-inch pan. In 3-quart saucepan, melt chocolate chips and butter over low heat, stirring frequently, until smooth; remove from heat. Cool slightly. Beat in sugar, vanilla and eggs with spoon. Stir in remaining ingredients except malted milk balls.
2. Spread batter in pan. Sprinkle with malted milk balls. Bake 30 to 35 minutes or until toothpick inserted in center comes out clean. Cool completely. Cut into 8 rows by 6 rows.

1 Brownie: Calories 100 (Calories from Fat 45); Total Fat 5g (Saturated Fat 2g); Cholesterol 15mg; Sodium 55mg; Total Carbohydrate 12g (Dietary Fiber 0g); Protein 2g

Malted milk powder is made from dehydrated milk and malted cereals. You can find it with the ice-cream toppings in the supermarket.

Caramel Candy Bars { 48 bars }

Prep Time: **25 Minutes** Start to Finish: **1 Hour 30 Minutes**

- 1 package (14 oz) vanilla caramels
- ⅓ cup milk
- 2 cups all-purpose flour
- 2 cups quick-cooking or old-fashioned oats
- 1½ cups packed brown sugar
- 1 teaspoon baking soda
- ½ teaspoon salt
- 1 egg
- 1 cup butter or margarine, softened
- 1 package (6 oz) semisweet chocolate chips (1 cup)
- 1 cup chopped walnuts or dry-roasted peanuts

1 Heat oven to 350°F. In 2-quart saucepan, heat caramels and milk over low heat, stirring frequently, until smooth; remove from heat.

2 In large bowl, mix flour, oats, brown sugar, baking soda and salt with spoon. Stir in egg and butter until mixture is crumbly. Press half of the crumbly mixture in ungreased 13 × 9-inch pan. Bake 10 minutes.

3 Sprinkle chocolate chips and walnuts over baked layer. Drizzle with caramel mixture. Sprinkle with remaining crumbly mixture; press gently into caramel mixture. Bake 20 to 25 minutes or until golden brown. Cool 30 minutes. Loosen edges from sides of pan. Cool completely. Cut into 8 rows by 6 rows.

1 Bar: Calories 155 (Calories from Fat 65); Total Fat 7g (Saturated Fat 2g); Cholesterol 5mg; Sodium 120mg; Total Carbohydrate 22g (Dietary Fiber 1g); Protein 2g

Pumpkin-Spice Bars with Cream Cheese Frosting

{ 49 bars }

Prep Time: **20 Minutes** Start to Finish: **2 Hours 50 Minutes**

BARS

4 eggs

2 cups granulated sugar

1 cup vegetable oil

1 can (15 oz) pumpkin (not pumpkin pie mix)

2 cups all-purpose flour

2 teaspoons baking powder

1 teaspoon baking soda

½ teaspoon salt

2 teaspoons ground cinnamon

½ teaspoon ground ginger

¼ teaspoon ground cloves

1 cup raisins, if desired

CREAM CHEESE FROSTING

1 package (8 oz) cream cheese, softened

¼ cup butter or margarine, softened

2 to 3 teaspoons milk

1 teaspoon vanilla

4 cups powdered sugar

½ cup chopped walnuts, if desired

1. Heat oven to 350°F. Spray 15 × 10 × 1-inch pan with cooking spray.
2. In large bowl, beat eggs, granulated sugar, oil and pumpkin with wire whisk until smooth. Stir in flour, baking powder, baking soda, salt, cinnamon, ginger and cloves. Stir in raisins. Spread in pan.
3. Bake 25 to 30 minutes or until toothpick inserted in center comes out clean and bars spring back when touched lightly in center. Cool completely, about 2 hours.
4. In medium bowl, beat cream cheese, butter, milk and vanilla with electric mixer on low speed until smooth. Gradually beat in powdered sugar, 1 cup at a time, on low speed until smooth and spreadable. Spread frosting over bars. Sprinkle with walnuts. For bars, cut into 7 rows by 7 rows. Store covered in refrigerator.

1 Bar: Calories 160 (Calories from Fat 70); Total Fat 8g (Saturated Fat 2.5g); Cholesterol 25mg; Sodium 95mg; Total Carbohydrate 23g (Dietary Fiber 0g); Protein 1g

Pecan Pie Squares

60 squares

Prep Time: **15 Minutes** Start to Finish: **2 Hours**

CRUST

3 cups all-purpose flour

¾ cup butter or margarine, softened

⅓ cup sugar

½ teaspoon salt

FILLING

4 eggs, slightly beaten

1½ cups sugar

1½ cups corn syrup

3 tablespoons butter or margarine, melted

1½ teaspoons vanilla

2½ cups chopped pecans

1. Heat oven to 350°F. Grease 15 × 10 × 1-inch pan. In large bowl, beat all crust ingredients with electric mixer on low speed until crumbly (mixture will be dry). Press firmly in pan. Bake about 20 minutes or until light golden brown.
2. In large bowl, mix all filling ingredients except pecans until well blended. Stir in pecans.
3. Pour filling over baked layer; spread evenly. Bake about 25 minutes or until filling is set. Cool completely. Cut into 10 rows by 6 rows.

1 Square: Calories 140 (Calories from Fat 65); Total Fat 7g (Saturated Fat 1g); Cholesterol 15mg; Sodium 65mg; Total Carbohydrate 18g (Dietary Fiber 0g); Protein 1g

Walnut Pie Squares are just as delicious and are made by substituting walnuts for the pecans.

Linzer Torte Bars { 48 bars }

Prep Time: **10 Minutes** Start to Finish: **1 Hour 35 Minutes**

- 1 cup all-purpose flour
- 1 cup powdered sugar
- 1 cup ground walnuts
- ½ cup butter or margarine, softened
- ½ teaspoon ground cinnamon
- ⅔ cup red raspberry preserves

1 Heat oven to 375°F. In large bowl, mix all ingredients except preserves with spoon until crumbly. Press two thirds of crumbly mixture in ungreased 9-inch square pan. Spread with preserves. Sprinkle with remaining crumbly mixture; press gently into preserves.

2 Bake 20 to 25 minutes or until light golden brown. Cool completely. For bars, cut into 8 rows by 6 rows.

1 Bar: Calories 60 (Calories from Fat 25); Total Fat 3g (Saturated Fat 0g); Cholesterol 0mg; Sodium 25mg; Total Carbohydrate 8g (Dietary Fiber 0g); Protein 0g

{ The flavors in this bar were inspired by linzertorte, a classic European dessert originating in Linz, Austria. Ground nuts, spices and raspberry preserves are quintessential to the namesake. }

Cardamom-Cashew Bars

48 bars

Prep Time: **20 Minutes** Start to Finish: **1 Hour 5 Minutes**

CRUST

½ package (8-oz size) ⅓-less-fat cream cheese (Neufchâtel)

½ cup powdered sugar

¼ cup packed brown sugar

2 teaspoons vanilla

1 egg yolk

1½ cups all-purpose flour

FILLING

1½ cups packed brown sugar

½ cup fat-free egg product or 2 eggs

3 tablespoons all-purpose flour

2 teaspoons vanilla

½ teaspoon ground cardamom or cinnamon

¼ teaspoon salt

1½ cups cashew pieces and halves

ORANGE DRIZZLE

¾ cup powdered sugar

1 tablespoon orange juice

1. Heat oven to 350°F. Grease 13 × 9-inch pan. To make crust: In medium bowl, beat cream cheese and sugars with electric mixer on medium speed until fluffy. Beat in vanilla and egg yolk. Gradually stir in flour to make a soft dough. Press dough evenly in pan. Bake 15 to 20 minutes or until very light brown.
2. In medium bowl, beat all filling ingredients except cashews with electric mixer on medium speed about 2 minutes or until thick and colored. Stir in cashews. Spread over baked crust.
3. Bake 19 to 22 minutes or until top is golden brown and bars are set around edges. Cool completely.
4. In small bowl, mix icing ingredients until smooth and spreadable. Spread over bars. For bars, cut into 8 rows by 6 rows.

1 Bar: Calories 90 (Calories from Fat 25); Total Fat 2.5g (Saturated Fat 0.5g); Cholesterol 5mg; Sodium 30mg; Total Carbohydrate 16g (Dietary Fiber 0g); Protein 1g

3

family favorites

Best Chocolate Chip Cookies

About 3½ dozen cookies

Prep Time: **1 Hour 25 Minutes** Start to Finish: **1 Hour 40 Minutes**

- 1½ cups butter or margarine (3 sticks), room temperature
- 1¼ cups granulated sugar
- 1¼ cups packed brown sugar
- 1 tablespoon vanilla
- 2 large eggs
- 4 cups all-purpose flour
- 2 teaspoons baking soda
- 1 teaspoon salt
- 1 bag (24 oz) semisweet chocolate chips (4 cups)
- 2 cups coarsely chopped nuts, if desired

1. Heat oven to 375°F. In large bowl, beat butter, both sugars, vanilla and eggs with electric mixer on medium speed (or with wooden spoon) until light and fluffy. Stir in flour, baking soda and salt (dough will be stiff). Stir in chocolate chips and nuts.
2. For each cookie, scoop dough with ¼-cup dry-ingredient measuring cup. Using back of knife or metal spatula, level dough even with top of cup. Push dough onto ungreased cookie sheet with spoon or rubber spatula, placing cookies 2 inches apart. Flatten slightly with fork.
3. Bake 12 to 15 minutes or until light brown (centers will be soft). Cool 1 to 2 minutes on cookie sheet, remove cookies to cooling rack, using turner. Cool cookie sheet 10 minutes between batches.

1 Cookie: Calories 210; Total Fat 10g; Cholesterol 25mg; Sodium 150mg; Total Carbohydrate 28g (Dietary Fiber 1g); Protein 2g

Candy Cookies Substitute 4 cups candy-coated chocolate candies for the chocolate chips.

Best Chocolate Chip Bars Press dough in ungreased 13 × 9-inch pan. Bake 15 to 20 minutes or until golden brown. Cool in pan on cooling rack. For 48 bars, cut into 8 rows by 6 rows.

Double-Frosted Chocolate Sandwich Cookies { 3 dozen cookies }

Prep Time: **45 Minutes** Start to Finish: **1 Hour 15 Minutes**

1 bag (12 oz) white vanilla baking chips

4 teaspoons shortening

1 package (14 oz) creme-filled chocolate sandwich cookies

1 bag (10 oz) mint-flavored chocolate chips

Candy decorations, colored glitter sugars or decorator sugar crystals

1 Line cookie sheet with waxed paper. In small microwavable bowl, microwave white baking chips and 2 teaspoons of the shortening uncovered on Medium 4 to 5 minutes or until mixture can be stirred smooth. Dip 18 of the cookies, one at a time, into white chip mixture; place on waxed paper. Refrigerate 5 to 10 minutes or until coating is set.

2 Meanwhile, in small microwavable bowl, microwave mint chocolate chips and remaining 2 teaspoons shortening uncovered on Medium 4 to 5 minutes or until mixture can be stirred smooth. Dip remaining cookies, one at a time, into chocolate mixture; place on waxed paper. Refrigerate 5 to 10 minutes or until coating is set.

3 Drizzle remaining melted chocolate mixture (reheat slightly if mixture has hardened) over tops of white-coated cookies; sprinkle with candy decorations. Drizzle remaining melted white mixture (reheat slightly if mixture has hardened) over tops of chocolate-coated cookies; sprinkle with candy decorations. Let stand about 10 minutes or until set.

1 Cookie: Calories 150 (Calories from Fat 70); Total Fat 8g (Saturated Fat 4g); Cholesterol 0mg; Sodium 85mg; Total Carbohydrate 18g (Dietary Fiber 1g); Protein 2g

Candy-Topped Blossom Cookies

{ 48 cookies }

Prep Time: **1 Hour 35 Minutes** Start to Finish: **2 Hours 5 Minutes**

- 1 can (14 oz) sweetened condensed milk (not evaporated)
- 1 cup creamy peanut butter
- 2 cups Original Bisquick® mix
- 1 teaspoon vanilla
- 3 tablespoons sugar
- 48 round chewy caramels in milk chocolate (from 12-oz bag), unwrapped

1 Heat oven to 375°F. In large bowl, beat condensed milk and peanut butter with electric mixer on medium speed until well blended.

2 Stir in Bisquick mix and vanilla until well blended.

3 Shape dough into 48 (1-inch) balls. Measure sugar into small bowl. Dip top of each ball into sugar. On ungreased cookie sheets, place balls 2 inches apart.

4 Bake 7 to 9 minutes. Firmly press 1 caramel into center of each cookie. Bake about 1 minute or until chocolate begins to soften and cookie begins to turn light golden brown. Cool 2 to 3 minutes. Remove from cookie sheet to cooling rack. Cool completely, about 30 minutes.

1 Cookie: Calories 110 (Calories from Fat 50); Total Fat 5g (Saturated Fat 2g); Cholesterol 0mg; Sodium 110mg; Total Carbohydrate 14g (Dietary Fiber 0g); Protein 2g

Get the kids involved in making this recipe. Simple steps and kid-friendly ingredients make for great holiday memories.

These cookies freeze well. Make them early in the season, cool completely and freeze in an airtight container.

Chocolate Spritz Reindeer

{ 5 dozen cookies }

Prep Time: **1 Hour** Start to Finish: **1 Hour 15 Minutes**

- 1 cup butter, softened
- ½ cup powdered sugar
- ½ cup packed brown sugar
- ¼ cup unsweetened baking cocoa
- 3 tablespoons milk
- 1 teaspoon vanilla
- 1 egg yolk
- 2 cups all-purpose flour
- 60 large pretzel twists
- 120 miniature candy-coated chocolate baking bits
- 60 miniature chocolate chips

1 Heat oven to 375°F. In large bowl, beat butter with electric mixer on medium speed until light and fluffy. Beat in sugars and cocoa until well blended. Beat in milk, vanilla and egg yolk. On low speed, slowly beat in flour until well blended, scraping bowl occasionally.

2 Fit heart template in cookie press; fill cookie press with dough. Place pretzels on lightly floured surface. Force dough through template on top of flat, bottom end of each pretzel twist (two rounds at top of pretzel will form the antlers). Press 2 baking bits at upper part of heart to make eyes, and 1 chocolate chip to make nose on each reindeer. Place reindeer on ungreased cookie sheet.

3 Bake 8 to 10 minutes or until cookies are firm, but not browned. Remove from pans to cooling rack. Cool completely, about 15 minutes.

1 Cookie: Calories 130 (Calories from Fat 40); Total Fat 4.5g (Saturated Fat 2.5g); Cholesterol 10mg; Sodium 240mg; Total Carbohydrate 21g (Dietary Fiber 1g); Protein 2g

{ If you don't have a cookie press, shape dough into 1¼-inch balls. Press 1 ball over bottom of 1 pretzel, pinching bottom in to form nose. }

Gingersnaps { About 4 dozen cookies }

Prep Time: **1 Hour 15 Minutes** Start to Finish: **2 Hours 45 Minutes**

- 1 cup packed brown sugar
- ¾ cup shortening
- ¼ cup molasses
- 1 egg
- 2¼ cups all-purpose flour
- 2 teaspoons baking soda
- 1 teaspoon ground cinnamon
- 1 teaspoon ground ginger
- ½ teaspoon ground cloves
- ¼ teaspoon salt
- Granulated sugar

1. In large bowl, beat brown sugar, shortening, molasses and egg with electric mixer on medium speed, or mix with spoon. Stir in remaining ingredients except granulated sugar. Cover; refrigerate at least 1 hour.
2. Heat oven to 375°F. Lightly grease cookie sheet with shortening or cooking spray.
3. In small bowl, place granulated sugar. Shape dough by rounded teaspoonfuls into balls; dip tops into granulated sugar. Place balls, sugared sides up, about 3 inches apart on cookie sheet.
4. Bake 9 to 12 minutes or just until set. Remove from cookie sheet to cooling rack. Cool completely, about 30 minutes.

1 Cookie: Calories 80 (Calories from Fat 30); Total Fat 3.5g (Saturated Fat 1g); Cholesterol 0mg; Sodium 70mg; Total Carbohydrate 11g (Dietary Fiber 0g); Protein 0g

Gingerbread Cookies with Royal Icing { 5 dozen cookies }

Prep Time: **1 Hour 40 Minutes** Start to Finish: **3 Hours 40 Minutes**

COOKIES

½ cup butter or margarine, softened

½ cup packed brown sugar

½ cup mild-flavor or full-flavor molasses

⅓ cup cold water

3½ cups all-purpose flour

2 teaspoons baking soda

2 teaspoons ground ginger

½ teaspoon ground allspice

½ teaspoon ground cinnamon

¼ teaspoon salt

¼ teaspoon ground cloves

ROYAL ICING

1 tablespoon meringue powder

2 tablespoons cold water

1 cup powdered sugar

Granulated sugar, if desired

1. In large bowl, beat butter, brown sugar, molasses and cold water with electric mixer on medium speed (or with wooden spoon) until well mixed. Mixture may look curdled. With wooden spoon, stir in remaining cookie ingredients until soft dough forms. Wrap with plastic wrap; refrigerate until firm, at least 2 hours.
2. Heat oven to 350°F. Lightly spray cookie sheets with cooking spray. On floured surface, roll dough ⅛ inch thick.
3. Cut dough with floured 3½ × 2½-inch gingerbread boy or girl cookie cutter or other cookie cutter. Place on cookie sheets 2 inches apart. Reroll dough, and cut additional cookies.
4. Bake 10 to 12 minutes or until no indentation remains when touched. Immediately remove from cookie sheets to cooling rack. Cool cookie sheets 10 minutes between batches. Cool cookies completely, about 30 minutes.
5. In medium bowl, beat meringue powder and cold water with electric mixer on medium speed until peaks form. Gradually beat in powdered sugar until soft peaks form, about 1 minute. Spoon icing into decorating bag fitted with medium round tip, and pipe over cookies. Sprinkle with sugar. Let stand about 5 minutes or until icing is set.

Look for meringue powder in the baking aisle of the grocery store.

1 Cookie: Calories 60 (Calories from Fat 15); Total Fat 1.5g (Saturated Fat 1g); Cholesterol 0mg; Sodium 65mg; Total Carbohydrate 12g (Dietary Fiber 0g); Protein 0g

Ginger-Ski Men

10 cookies

Prep Time: 1 Hour **Start to Finish:** 1 Hour

- 30 fruit-flavored ring-shaped gummy candies (from 7-oz package)
- 10 (2½-inch) gingerbread man cookies (from 5-oz package)
- 1 roll chewy fruit-flavored snack (from 6-roll box)
- 20 pretzel sticks
- 1 cup white vanilla baking chips
- 20 red cinnamon candies
- 20 miniature chocolate chips
- 10 gingersnap cookies (from 16-oz box)
- 20 (3-inch) candy canes

1. Cover work space with large sheet of waxed paper. Gently stretch 1 candy ring, and pull over top of 1 gingerbread man's head to make hat; repeat 9 times. Unroll fruit snack; cut into 5-inch pieces, separating along perforations. Wrap 1 (5-inch) piece around neck, twisting in center of each, to make scarf. Gently press to stick. Place 1 candy ring near 1 end of each pretzel stick to make ski poles.
2. Place white vanilla baking chips in small resealable freezer plastic bag. Microwave on High 45 seconds, turning bag over after 30 seconds. Squeeze bag until chips are melted and smooth (if necessary, continue microwaving, 15 seconds at a time, until smooth). Cut small tip off one corner of bag.
3. Using melted chips as glue, squeeze small dot in middle of face; attach 1 cinnamon candy to make nose. Squeeze 2 small dots above nose; attach 2 miniature chocolate chips to make eyes. Squeeze small amount to hold candy rings onto pretzels at bottom. Squeeze small amount on top of head to hold candy ring; place cinnamon candy on top. Squeeze small amount to make each hand, and attach pretzel ski poles, setting outward to fit outside skis. Drizzle over top of round gingersnap cookie, and set 2 miniature candy canes ½ inch apart, with hook ends standing up. Repeat for remaining ski men. Allow to set, about 30 minutes.

4 When set, microwave chips in bag to melt again, about 30 seconds or until smooth. For each ski man, squeeze small amount on top of candy cane skis; stand gingerbread man on each; allow to set, about 30 minutes.

1 Cookie: Calories 390 (Calories from Fat 110); Total Fat 12g (Saturated Fat 6g); Cholesterol 0mg; Sodium 270mg; Total Carbohydrate 66g (Dietary Fiber 1g); Protein 4g

"Lollipop" Cookies { About 2 dozen cookies }

Prep Time: **15 Minutes** Start to Finish: **3 Hours 15 Minutes**

COOKIES

1 box (12.8 oz) Rice Chex® or 1 box (14 oz) Corn Chex® cereal

1 bag (16 oz) large marshmallows (about 64)

¼ cup butter or margarine

About 24 wooden sticks with rounded ends or cookie sticks, if desired

Creamy Vanilla Glaze, if desired

Gumdrops, if desired

CREAMY VANILLA GLAZE

1 cup powdered sugar

½ teaspoon vanilla

1 tablespoon water or 1 to 2 tablespoons milk

1 Butter 15 × 10 × 1-inch pan.

2 In large microwavable bowl, microwave marshmallows and butter on High 2 to 3 minutes, stirring every minute, until mixture is smooth. Stir in cereal. Using buttered back of spoon or hands, press firmly in pan. Cool 2 to 3 hours before cutting into shapes.

3 Cut into shapes with 2½- to 3-inch holiday cutters (such as snowmen, stars, Christmas trees, etc.) that have been lightly sprayed with cooking spray. Insert wooden stick about 1 inch into bottom of each shape; reshape cutouts as needed.

4 In small bowl, mix all glaze ingredients with spoon until smooth and spreadable. Decorate cookies with glaze and gumdrops.

1 Cookie: Calories 170 (Calories from Fat 40); Total Fat 4g (Saturated Fat 2g); Cholesterol 10mg; Sodium 200mg; Total Carbohydrate 31g (Dietary Fiber 0g); Protein 2g

Chocolate Brownies { 16 brownies }

Prep Time: 25 Minutes **Start to Finish:** 3 Hours 10 Minutes

- 5 oz unsweetened baking chocolate
- ⅔ cup butter or margarine
- 1¾ cups granulated sugar
- 2 teaspoons vanilla
- 3 eggs
- 1 cup all-purpose flour
- 1 cup chopped walnuts, if desired

1. Heat oven to 350°F. Spray bottom and sides of 9-inch square pan with cooking spray.
2. Cut baking chocolate into pieces. In 1-quart saucepan, melt chocolate and butter over low heat, stirring constantly, just until chocolate is melted. Remove from heat; cool 5 minutes.
3. In medium bowl, beat sugar, vanilla and eggs with electric mixer on high speed 5 minutes. On low speed, beat in chocolate mixture, stopping occasionally to scrape batter from side and bottom of bowl with rubber spatula. Beat in flour, stopping occasionally to scrape bowl, just until mixed. Stir in walnuts. Spread batter evenly in pan.
4. Bake 40 to 45 minutes or just until brownies begin to pull away from sides of pan. Be sure not to overbake brownies because edges will get hard and dry. Cool in pan on cooling rack about 2 hours until completely cooled. Cut into 4 rows by 4 rows.

1 Brownie: Calories 240; Total Fat 12g; Cholesterol 55mg; Sodium 55mg; Total Carbohydrate 31g; (Dietary Fiber 1g); Protein 3g

Chocolate–Peanut Butter Brownies Substitute ⅓ cup crunchy peanut butter for ⅓ cup of the butter. Omit walnuts. Before baking, arrange 16 one-inch chocolate-covered peanut butter cup candies, unwrapped, over top. Press into batter so tops of cups are even with top of batter.

Peanut Butter and Jam Bars { 32 bars }

Prep Time: **25 Minutes** Start to Finish: **45 Minutes**

BARS

½ cup granulated sugar

½ cup packed brown sugar

½ cup shortening

½ cup peanut butter

1 egg

1¼ cups all-purpose flour

¾ teaspoon baking soda

½ teaspoon baking powder

½ cup red raspberry jam

VANILLA DRIZZLE

2 tablespoons butter or margarine

1 cup powdered sugar

1 teaspoon vanilla

3 to 4 teaspoons hot water

1. Heat oven to 350°F. In large bowl, beat sugars, shortening, peanut butter and egg with electric mixer on medium speed, or mix with spoon. Stir in flour, baking soda and baking powder.
2. Reserve 1 cup dough. In ungreased 13 × 9-inch pan, press remaining dough. Spread with jam. Crumble reserved dough and sprinkle over jam; gently press into jam. Bake 20 to 25 minutes or until golden brown. Cool completely.
3. In 1-quart saucepan, melt butter over low heat; remove from heat. Stir in powdered sugar and vanilla. Stir in hot water, 1 teaspoon at a time, until smooth and thin enough to drizzle. Cut into 8 rows by 4 rows.

1 Bar: Calories 135 (Calories from Fat 55); Total Fat 6g (Saturated Fat 1g); Cholesterol 5mg; Sodium 70mg; Total Carbohydrate 18g (Dietary Fiber 0g); Protein 2g

No-Bake Peanut Butter Squares

{ 36 squares }

Prep Time: **20 Minutes** Start to Finish: **50 Minutes**

- 1½ cups powdered sugar
- 1 cup graham cracker crumbs (about 12 squares)
- ½ cup butter or margarine
- ½ cup peanut butter
- 1 cup white vanilla baking chips or semisweet chocolate chips (6 oz)
- Candy decorations, if desired

1. In medium bowl, mix powdered sugar and cracker crumbs. In 1-quart saucepan, heat butter and peanut butter over low heat, stirring occasionally, until melted. Stir into crumb mixture. Press in ungreased 8-inch square pan.
2. In 1-quart saucepan, melt white vanilla baking chips over low heat, stirring frequently. Spread over crumb mixture. Immediately sprinkle with candy decorations. Refrigerate about 30 minutes or until firm.
3. For squares, cut into 6 rows by 6 rows. (To cut diamond shapes, first cut straight parallel lines 1 to 1½ inches apart down the length of the pan. Second, cut diagonal lines 1 to 1½ inches apart across the straight cuts.) Store loosely covered in refrigerator.

1 Square: Calories 100 (Calories from Fat 50); Total Fat 6g (Saturated Fat 2.5g); Cholesterol 5mg; Sodium 45mg; Total Carbohydrate 10g (Dietary Fiber 0g); Protein 1g

No-Bake Honey-Oat Bars { 24 bars }

Prep Time: **10 Minutes** Start to Finish: **10 Minutes**

- ¼ cup sugar
- ¼ cup butter or margarine
- ⅓ cup honey
- ½ teaspoon ground cinnamon
- 1 cup diced dried fruit and raisin mixture
- 1½ cups Wheaties® cereal
- 1 cup quick-cooking oats
- ½ cup sliced almonds

1. Butter 9-inch square pan. In 3-quart saucepan, heat sugar, butter, honey and cinnamon to boiling over medium heat, stirring constantly. Boil 1 minute, stirring constantly; remove from heat. Stir in dried fruit. Stir in remaining ingredients.
2. Press mixture in pan with back of wooden spoon. Cool completely. Cut into 6 rows by 4 rows.

1 Bar: Calories 85 (Calories from Fat 25); Total Fat 3g (Saturated Fat 1g); Cholesterol 0mg; Sodium 35mg; Total Carbohydrate 14g (Dietary Fiber 1g); Protein 1g

Confetti Caramel Bars { 32 bars }

Prep Time: **15 Minutes** Start to Finish: **3 Hours 5 Minutes**

- 1 cup packed brown sugar
- 1 cup butter or margarine, softened
- 1½ teaspoons vanilla
- 1 egg
- 2 cups all-purpose flour
- ½ cup light corn syrup
- 2 tablespoons butter or margarine
- 1 cup butterscotch-flavored chips
- 1½ to 2 cups assorted candies and nuts (such as candy corn, candy-coated chocolate candies and salted peanuts)

1. Heat oven to 350°F. In large bowl, beat brown sugar, 1 cup butter, the vanilla and egg with electric mixer on medium speed, or mix with spoon. Stir in flour. Press evenly in bottom of ungreased 13 × 9-inch pan. Bake 20 to 22 minutes or until light brown. Cool 20 minutes.
2. In 1-quart saucepan, heat corn syrup, 2 tablespoons butter and the butterscotch chips over medium heat, stirring occasionally, until chips are melted; remove from heat. Cool 10 minutes.
3. Spread butterscotch mixture over baked crust. Sprinkle with candies and nuts; gently press into butterscotch mixture. Cover; refrigerate at least 2 hours until butterscotch mixture is firm. For bars, cut into 8 rows by 4 rows.

1 Bar: Calories 200 (Calories from Fat 90); Total Fat 10g (Saturated Fat 5g); Cholesterol 25mg; Sodium 70mg; Total Carbohydrate 26g (Dietary Fiber 0g); Protein 2g

{ A simple pan of bars can look extraordinary if you cut them into triangles or diamonds, and place the serving plate on confetti. }

4

extra-special cookies and bars

Chocolate-Cherry Tea Cookies

{ About 4 dozen cookies }

Prep Time: **1 Hour 25 Minutes** Start to Finish: **2 Hours 5 Minutes**

- 1 cup butter, softened
- 1 cup powdered sugar
- ½ teaspoon almond extract
- 2 cups all-purpose flour
- ¼ teaspoon salt
- 1 cup (8 oz) candied cherries, finely chopped
- ½ cup dark chocolate chips

1. Heat oven to 400°F. In large bowl, beat butter with electric mixer on medium speed until fluffy. Gradually beat in ½ cup of the powdered sugar until light and fluffy. Stir in almond extract. In medium bowl, mix flour and salt. On low speed, beat flour mixture into butter mixture until well blended. Stir in cherries.
2. Shape dough into 1-inch balls. On ungreased cookie sheet, place balls 2 inches apart.
3. Bake 9 to 11 minutes or until edges just begin to brown. Cool slightly. In small bowl, place remaining ½ cup powdered sugar. Roll each cookie in powdered sugar. Place on cooling rack to cool completely.
4. Place chocolate chips in small resealable freezer plastic bag. Microwave on High 45 to 60 seconds, turning bag over every 20 seconds. Squeeze bag until chips are melted and smooth. Cut small tip off one corner of bag, and drizzle over cooled cookies. Let stand at room temperature at least 30 minutes until chocolate hardens before storing.

1 Cookie: Calories 90 (Calories from Fat 40); Total Fat 4.5g (Saturated Fat 3g); Cholesterol 10mg; Sodium 45mg; Total Carbohydrate 11g (Dietary Fiber 0g); Protein 0g

Espresso Thumbprint Cookies

{ About 3½ dozen cookies }

Prep Time: **1 Hour 30 Minutes** Start to Finish: **1 Hour 45 Minutes**

COOKIES

¾ cup sugar

¾ cup butter or margarine, softened

½ teaspoon vanilla

1 egg

1¾ cups all-purpose flour

3 tablespoons unsweetened baking cocoa

¼ teaspoon salt

ESPRESSO FILLING

¼ cup whipping cream

2 teaspoons instant espresso coffee (dry)

1 cup (half 11.5-oz bag) milk chocolate chips

1 tablespoon coffee-flavored liqueur, if desired

Candy sprinkles or crushed hard peppermint candies, if desired

1 Heat oven to 350°F. In large bowl, beat sugar, butter, vanilla and egg with electric mixer on medium speed, or mix with spoon. Stir in flour, cocoa and salt.

2 Shape dough by rounded teaspoonfuls into 1-inch balls. On ungreased cookie sheet, place balls about 2 inches apart. Press thumb or end of wooden spoon into center of each cookie to make indentation, but do not press all the way to the cookie sheet.

3 Bake 7 to 11 minutes or until edges are firm. Quickly remake indentations with end of wooden spoon if necessary. Immediately remove from cookie sheet to cooling rack. Cool completely, about 30 minutes.

4 Meanwhile, in 1-quart saucepan, heat whipping cream and coffee (dry) over medium heat, stirring occasionally, until steaming and coffee is dissolved. Remove from heat; stir in chocolate chips until melted. Stir in liqueur. Cool about 10 minutes or until thickened. Spoon rounded ½ teaspoon filling into indentation in each cookie. Top with candy sprinkles.

1 Cookie: Calories 90 (Calories from Fat 45); Total Fat 5g (Saturated Fat 2.5g); Cholesterol 15mg; Sodium 40mg; Total Carbohydrate 10g (Dietary Fiber 0g); Protein 1g

Rum-Cashew Biscotti

About 3 dozen biscotti

Prep Time: **25 Minutes** Start to Finish: **2 Hours**

BISCOTTI

⅔ cup granulated sugar

½ cup vegetable oil

2 teaspoons rum extract

2 eggs

2½ cups all-purpose flour

1 cup unsalted cashew pieces

1 teaspoon baking powder

¼ teaspoon baking soda

¼ teaspoon salt

RUM GLAZE

½ cup powdered sugar

2 teaspoons eggnog or half-and-half

1 teaspoon rum or ½ teaspoon rum extract

1. Heat oven to 350°F. In large bowl, beat granulated sugar, oil, 2 teaspoons rum extract and the eggs with spoon. Stir in remaining biscotti ingredients.
2. Turn dough onto lightly floured surface. Knead until smooth. On ungreased cookie sheet, shape half of dough at a time into 10 × 3-inch rectangle.
3. Bake 25 to 30 minutes or until toothpick inserted in center comes out clean. Cool on cookie sheet 15 minutes. Cut crosswise into ½-inch slices. Place slices, cut sides down, on cookie sheet.
4. Bake about 15 minutes, turning once, until crisp and light brown. Immediately remove from cookie sheet to cooling rack. Cool completely, about 45 minutes. In small bowl, mix all glaze ingredients with spoon until smooth and thin enough to drizzle. Drizzle glaze over biscotti.

1 Biscotti: Calories 110 (Calories from Fat 45); Total Fat 5g (Saturated Fat 1g;); Cholesterol 10mg; Sodium 45mg; Total Carbohydrate 13g (Dietary Fiber 0g); Protein 2g

Chocolate-Dipped Biscotti Heat 3 oz semisweet baking chocolate or white chocolate baking bar and ½ teaspoon shortening until melted and smooth. Drizzle chocolate over biscotti, or dip half of each biscotti into melted chocolate. Immediately sprinkle with your choice of crushed hard peppermint candy, chopped pistachio or other nuts, decorator sugar crystals, chopped candied ginger or holiday candy decorations. Place on waxed paper until chocolate is set.

Holiday Melting Moments

About 3½ dozen cookies

Prep Time: **1 Hour 15 Minutes** Start to Finish: **2 Hours 45 Minutes**

COOKIES

1 cup butter, softened (do not use margarine)

1 egg yolk

1 cup plus 2 tablespoons all-purpose flour

½ cup cornstarch

½ cup powdered sugar

2 tablespoons unsweetened baking cocoa

⅛ teaspoon salt

VANILLA FROSTING

1 cup powdered sugar

2 tablespoons butter or margarine, softened

1 teaspoon vanilla

2 to 3 teaspoons milk

2 candy canes, about 6 inches long, finely crushed

1 In large bowl, beat 1 cup butter and egg yolk with electric mixer on medium speed, or mix with spoon. Stir in remaining cookie ingredients. Cover; refrigerate about 1 hour or until firm.

2 Heat oven to 375°F. Shape dough into 1-inch balls. On ungreased cookie sheet, place balls about 2 inches apart.

3 Bake 10 to 12 minutes or until set but not brown. Remove from cookie sheet to cooling rack. Cool completely, about 30 minutes.

4 In small bowl, mix all frosting ingredients except candy canes with spoon until smooth and spreadable. Frost cookies; sprinkle with crushed candy canes.

1 Cookie: Calories 80 (Calories from Fat 45); Total Fat 5g (Saturated Fat 2.5g); Cholesterol 20mg; Sodium 40mg; Total Carbohydrate 9g (Dietary Fiber 0g); Protein 0g

Pecan-Shortbread Trees { 32 cookies }

Prep Time: **30 Minutes** Start to Finish: **1 Hour 15 Minutes**

1 cup butter, softened

⅔ cup powdered sugar

½ teaspoon vanilla

5 drops green food color

1¾ cups all-purpose flour

½ cup coarsely chopped pecans

32 pecan halves

¾ cup white vanilla baking chips

Granulated sugar, if desired

32 yellow decorating stars, if desired

1. Heat oven to 325°F. Spray or lightly grease 2 large cookie sheets. In large bowl, beat butter and powdered sugar with electric mixer on medium speed until light and fluffy. Beat in vanilla and food color. On low speed, beat in flour just until mixed. Stir in chopped pecans.
2. Divide dough into 4 equal parts; shape each into ball. Place 2 balls of dough on each cookie sheet, on opposite ends. With rolling pin or floured fingers, gently flatten and shape each ball into 6-inch circle. With large knife, divide and cut each round into 8 wedges, slightly separating each cut with knife. Poke tops of wedges with fork, and place 1 pecan half in middle of each outer edge to make tree trunk.
3. Bake 15 to 18 minutes or until firm but not brown. While still warm, cut into wedges again. Cool completely on cookie sheets, about 30 minutes.
4. Place cooled tree wedges on cooling racks or waxed paper. Place baking chips in small resealable freezer plastic bag. Microwave on High 40 to 60 seconds, turning bag over after 30 seconds. Squeeze bag gently until chips are melted and smooth. Cut small tip off one corner of bag, and drizzle side to side over wedges to make tree garland. Sprinkle with sugar. Top each tree with star.

1 Cookie: Calories 160 (Calories from Fat 100); Total Fat 11g (Saturated Fat 6g); Cholesterol 15mg; Sodium 65mg; Total Carbohydrate 15g (Dietary Fiber 0g); Protein 1g

After the holiday season, make these cookies without the food color, pecan "trunks" and stars.

If using paste food color, you need only a small amount to get a nice green color.

Sparkling Lemon Snowflakes

{ 6 dozen cookies }

Prep Time: **50 Minutes** Start to Finish: **1 Hour 40 Minutes**

COOKIES

¾ cup butter, softened

¾ cup granulated sugar

2 teaspoons grated lemon peel

1 egg

2¼ cups all-purpose flour

¼ teaspoon salt

GLAZE

2 cups powdered sugar

2 tablespoons lemon juice

2 tablespoons water

¼ cup coarse white sparkling sugar

1. In large bowl, beat butter and granulated sugar with electric mixer on medium speed until light and fluffy. Add lemon peel and egg; beat until well blended. On low speed, gradually beat in flour and salt until well blended.
2. Heat oven to 350°F. On floured surface, roll dough ⅛ inch thick. Cut with lightly floured 2½- to 3-inch snowflake-shaped cookie cutter. On ungreased cookie sheets, place 2 inches apart.
3. Bake 8 to 10 minutes or until cookies just begin to brown. Remove from cookie sheets to cooling racks. Cool completely, about 10 minutes.
4. In small bowl, mix powdered sugar, lemon juice and water. Using small metal spatula, spread glaze on tops of cookies; sprinkle with sparkling sugar. When glaze is dry, store in airtight container.

1 Cookie: Calories 60 (Calories from Fat 20); Total Fat 2g (Saturated Fat 1g); Cholesterol 10mg; Sodium 25mg; Total Carbohydrate 9g (Dietary Fiber 0g); Protein 0g

If you don't have a snowflake-shaped cookie cutter, you can use either a star-shaped or scalloped-edge cutter. Just cut small triangles and pieces out of the center to form snowflakes.

Look for coarse sugar in the baking aisle of the supermarket, or search for it on sweetc.com.

Toffee Bars { 32 bars }

Prep Time: 15 Minutes Start to Finish: 1 Hour 20 Minutes

- 1 cup butter or margarine, softened
- 1 cup packed brown sugar
- 1 teaspoon vanilla
- 1 egg yolk
- 2 cups all-purpose flour
- ¼ teaspoon salt
- ⅔ cup milk chocolate chips
- ½ cup chopped nuts, if desired

1. Heat oven to 350°F. Spray 13 × 9-inch pan with cooking spray. In large bowl, mix butter, brown sugar, vanilla and egg yolk. Stir in flour and salt. Press in pan.
2. Bake 25 to 30 minutes or until very light brown (crust will be soft). Immediately sprinkle chocolate chips on hot crust. Let stand about 5 minutes or until chocolate is soft; spread evenly. Sprinkle with nuts.
3. Cool 30 minutes in pan on cooling rack. For bars, cut into 8 rows by 4 rows.

1 Bar: Calories 130 (Calories from Fat 60); Total Fat 7g (Saturated Fat 4g); Cholesterol 20mg; Sodium 65mg; Total Carbohydrate 15g (Dietary Fiber 0g); Protein 1g

Three bars (1.55 oz each) milk chocolate candy, broken into small pieces, can be substituted for the milk chocolate chips.

For easiest cutting, cut the bars while they're still warm.

Irish Cream Bars { 24 bars }

Prep Time: **20 Minutes** Start to Finish: **2 Hours 50 Minutes**

- ¾ cup all-purpose flour
- ½ cup butter or margarine, softened
- ¼ cup powdered sugar
- 2 tablespoons unsweetened baking cocoa
- ¾ cup sour cream
- ½ cup granulated sugar
- ⅓ cup Irish cream liqueur
- 1 tablespoon all-purpose flour
- 1 teaspoon vanilla
- 1 egg
- ½ cup whipping cream
- Chocolate sprinkles, if desired

1 Heat oven to 350°F. In small bowl, mix ¾ cup flour, the butter, powdered sugar and cocoa with spoon until soft dough forms. Press in bottom of ungreased 8- or 9-inch square pan. Bake 10 minutes.

2 In medium bowl, beat remaining ingredients except whipping cream and chocolate sprinkles with wire whisk until blended. Pour over baked layer. Bake 15 to 20 minutes or until filling is set. Cool slightly; refrigerate at least 2 hours before cutting.

3 For bars, cut into 6 rows by 4 rows. In chilled small bowl, beat whipping cream with electric mixer on high speed until stiff peaks form. Spoon whipped cream into decorating bag fitted with medium writing or star tip. Pipe dollop of cream onto each bar. Top with chocolate sprinkles. Store covered in refrigerator up to 48 hours.

1 Bar: Calories 110 (Calories from Fat 70); Total Fat 7g (Saturated Fat 4g); Cholesterol 35mg; Sodium 35mg; Total Carbohydrate 10g (Dietary Fiber 0g); Protein 1g

{ Instead of the Irish cream liqueur, substitute ⅓ cup Irish cream nondairy creamer (or ¼ cup half-and-half plus 2 tablespoons cold coffee and 1 teaspoon almond extract). }

Brandy Crème Brûlée Bars { 36 bars }

Prep Time: **25 Minutes** Start to Finish: **2 Hours 5 Minutes**

- 1 cup all-purpose flour
- ½ cup sugar
- ½ cup butter or margarine, softened
- 5 egg yolks
- ¼ cup sugar
- 1¼ cups whipping cream
- 1 tablespoon plus 1 teaspoon brandy or 1½ teaspoons brandy extract
- ⅓ cup sugar

1 Heat oven to 350°F. In small bowl, mix flour, ½ cup sugar and the butter with spoon. Press on bottom and ½ inch up sides of ungreased 9-inch square pan. Bake 20 minutes.

2 Reduce oven temperature to 300°F. In small bowl, beat egg yolks and ¼ cup sugar with spoon until thick. Gradually stir in whipping cream and brandy. Pour over baked layer.

3 Bake 40 to 50 minutes or until custard is set and knife inserted in center comes out clean. Cool completely, about 30 minutes. For bars, cut into 6 rows by 6 rows. Place bars on cookie sheet lined with waxed paper.

4 In heavy 1-quart saucepan, heat ⅓ cup sugar over medium heat until sugar begins to melt. Stir until sugar is completely dissolved and caramel colored. Cool slightly until caramel has thickened slightly. Drizzle hot caramel over bars. (If caramel begins to harden, return to medium heat and stir until thin enough to drizzle.) After caramel on bars has hardened, cover and refrigerate bars up to 48 hours.

1 Bar: Calories 90 (Calories from Fat 50); Total Fat 6g (Saturated Fat 3g); Cholesterol 45mg; Sodium 20mg; Total Carbohydrate 9g (Dietary Fiber 0g); Protein 0g

Strawberry–Almond Paste Shortbread Bars { 32 bars }

Prep Time: **25 Minutes** Start to Finish: **1 Hour 15 Minutes**

- 1 cup butter, softened
- ¾ cup granulated sugar
- 2 cups all-purpose flour
- ¼ teaspoon salt
- ¼ cup packed almond paste (from 7-oz roll), crumbled (not marzipan)
- ¼ cup sliced almonds
- 1 jar (12 oz) strawberry preserves
- 1 teaspoon powdered sugar

1. Heat oven to 350°F. Line bottom and sides of 9-inch square pan with foil, leaving 1 inch of foil overhanging at 2 opposite sides of pan. Spray foil with cooking spray.
2. In large bowl, beat butter and granulated sugar with electric mixer on medium-high speed until well mixed. Beat in flour and salt on medium speed just until blended. Press 3½ cups mixture into pan. Bake about 20 minutes or until top begins to brown.
3. Meanwhile, in same bowl, mix remaining crumb mixture and crumbled almond paste with fork until small clumps form. Stir in almonds.
4. Spread preserves evenly over hot base. Crumble almond paste mixture evenly over preserves; press slightly.
5. Bake 25 to 30 minutes or until top and edges are golden brown and preserves are bubbly. Using foil handles, lift bars from pan; remove foil from sides of bars. Cool completely on cooling rack before cutting. Sprinkle powdered sugar on top. For bars, cut into 8 rows by 4 rows. Cut each square in half diagonally.

1 Bar: Calories 140 (Calories from Fat 60); Total Fat 7g (Saturated Fat 3.5g); Cholesterol 15mg; Sodium 65mg; Total Carbohydrate 19g (Dietary Fiber 0g); Protein 1g

{ For a how-to photo and a simple technique for lining a pan with foil, see page 8. }

Holiday Eggnog Bars { 36 bars }

Prep Time: **15 Minutes** Start to Finish: **2 Hours 5 Minutes**

- ½ cup butter, softened
- ¾ cup sugar
- 1 cup all-purpose flour
- 5 egg yolks
- 1¼ cups whipping cream
- 1 tablespoon rum or 1 teaspoon rum extract
- ¾ teaspoon ground nutmeg

1. Heat oven to 350°F. Line bottom and sides of 9-inch square pan with foil, leaving 1 inch of foil overhanging at 2 opposite sides of pan. In small bowl, stir together butter, ½ cup of the sugar and the flour. Press in bottom and ½ inch up sides of pan. Bake 20 minutes.
2. Reduce oven temperature to 300°F. In small bowl, beat egg yolks and remaining ¼ cup sugar with electric mixer on medium-high speed until thick. Gradually beat in cream, rum and ¼ teaspoon of the nutmeg. Pour over baked layer.
3. Bake 40 to 50 minutes at 300°F until custard is set and knife inserted in center comes out clean. Cool completely, about 1 hour.
4. Sprinkle tops of bars evenly with remaining ½ teaspoon nutmeg. Using foil handles, lift cooled bars from pan to cutting board; remove foil from sides of bars. With sharp knife, cut into 6 rows by 6 rows. Cover; store in refrigerator.

1 Bar: Calories 80 (Calories from Fat 50); Total Fat 6g (Saturated Fat 3.5g); Cholesterol 45mg; Sodium 20mg; Total Carbohydrate 7g (Dietary Fiber 0g); Protein 1g

Don't like to drink plain eggnog but like the flavor? Then you're sure to love these squares for a holiday dessert.

Use an egg separator to easily separate the yolk from the egg white.

Chocolate-Raspberry Triangles

{ 4 dozen triangles }

Prep Time: **20 Minutes** Start to Finish: **2 Hours 10 Minutes**

- 1½ cups all-purpose flour
- ¾ cup sugar
- ¾ cup butter or margarine, softened
- 1 box (10 oz) frozen raspberries in syrup, thawed, undrained
- ¼ cup orange juice
- 1 tablespoon cornstarch
- ¾ miniature semisweet chocolate chips

1 Heat oven to 350°F. In medium bowl, mix flour, sugar, and butter with spoon. In bottom of ungreased 13 × 9-inch pan, press dough evenly. Bake 15 minutes.

2 In 1-quart saucepan, mix raspberries, orange juice and cornstarch. Heat to boiling, stirring constantly. Boil and stir 1 minute. Cool 10 minutes. Sprinkle chocolate chips over crust. Carefully spread raspberry mixture over chocolate chips.

3 Bake about 20 minutes or until raspberry mixture is set. Refrigerate about 1 hour or until chocolate is firm. For triangles, cut into 4 rows by 3 rows, then cut each square into 4 triangles.

1 Triangle: Calories 80 (Calories from Fat 35); Total Fat 4g (Saturated Fat 2g); Cholesterol 10mg; Sodium 20mg; Carbohydrate 10g (Dietary Fiber 1g); Protein 1g

metric conversion guide

volume

U.S. Units	Canadian Metric	Australian Metric
¼ teaspoon	1 mL	1 ml
½ teaspoon	2 mL	2 ml
1 teaspoon	5 mL	5 ml
1 tablespoon	15 mL	20 ml
¼ cup	50 mL	60 ml
⅓ cup	75 mL	80 ml
½ cup	125 mL	125 ml
⅔ cup	150 mL	170 ml
¾ cup	175 mL	190 ml
1 cup	250 mL	250 ml
1 quart	1 liter	1 liter
1½ quarts	1.5 liters	1.5 liters
2 quarts	2 liters	2 liters
2½ quarts	2.5 liters	2.5 liters
3 quarts	3 liters	3 liters
4 quarts	4 liters	4 liters

weight

U.S. Units	Canadian Metric	Australian Metric
1 ounce	30 grams	30 grams
2 ounces	55 grams	60 grams
3 ounces	85 grams	90 grams
4 ounces (¼ pound)	115 grams	125 grams
8 ounces (½ pound)	225 grams	225 grams
16 ounces (1 pound)	455 grams	500 grams
1 pound	455 grams	0.5 kilogram

NOTE: The recipes in this cookbook have not been developed or tested using metric measures. When converting recipes to metric, some variations in quality may be noted.

measurements

Inches	Centimeters
1	2.5
2	5.0
3	7.5
4	10.0
5	12.5
6	15.0
7	17.5
8	20.5
9	23.0
10	25.5
11	28.0
12	30.5
13	33.0

temperatures

Fahrenheit	Celsius
32°	0°
212°	100°
250°	120°
275°	140°
300°	150°
325°	160°
350°	180°
375°	190°
400°	200°
425°	220°
450°	230°
475°	240°
500°	260°

Recipe Index

Best Chocolate Chip Cookies 54
Brandy Crème Brûlée Bars 89
Butterscotch-Oatmeal Cookies 17
Candy-Topped Blossom Cookies 56
Caramel Candy Bars 45
Cardamom-Cashew Bars 50
Carrot-Spice Cookies 20
Chewy Orange-Date Bars 30
Chocolate Brownies 68
Chocolate-Cherry Tea Cookies 76
Chocolate Chip and Peanut Butter Cookies 16
Chocolate-Raspberry Triangles 94
Chocolate Spritz Reindeer 58
Confetti Caramel Bars 73
Double-Frosted Chocolate Sandwich Cookies 55
Espresso Thumbprint Cookies 78
Fudge Crinkles 12
Fudgy Pecan Bars 24
German Chocolate Bars 26
Gingerbread Cookies with Royal Icing 62
Ginger-Ski Men 64–65
Gingersnaps 60
Hidden Treasure Cookies 36
Holiday Eggnog Bars 92
Holiday Melting Moments 80
Inside-Out Chocolate Chip Cookies 34
Irish Cream Bars 88
Lemon Cheesecake Bars 28
Lemon Stampers 42
Linzer Torte Bars 49
"Lollipop" Cookies 66
Marvelously Minty Cookies 35
Milk Chocolate–Malt Brownies 44
No-Bake Honey-Oat Bars 72
No-Bake Peanut Butter Squares 70
Peanut Butter and Jam Bars 69
Peanutty Granola Cookies 14
Pecan Pie Squares 48
Pecan-Shortbread Trees 82
Peppermint Shortbread Bites 22
Pumpkin-Spice Bars with Cream Cheese Frosting 46
Rum-Cashew Biscotti 79
Season's Best Sugar Cookies 40
Sparkling Lemon Snowflakes 84
Spicy Pumpkin Cookies 18
Spritz 38
Strawberry–Almond Paste Shortbread Bars 90
Super-Easy Macaroon Chewies 19
Toffee Bars 86
Triple-Chocolate Cherry Bars 25
White Chocolate–Cranberry Bars 29